STORY 4
OF THE
GUARDIAN PRINCESSES

This book was produced by the collective work of the Guardian Princess Alliance.

Written by Setsu Shigematsu

Editorial Collective:
Ashanti McMillon
Kelsey Moore
Ilse Ackerman
Nasreen Popat
Nausheen Sheikh
Juliann Anesi
Pavita Singh

Songs by Ashanti McMillon
Princess Ten Ten's character and story inspired by Neill Chua and Jessica Yamane

Illustrated by A. Das
Original character design by Angela Eir, Nicole Phung, and Kayla Madison
Preliminary sketches by Krishna Das and Nicole Phung
Art assistance by Nicole Phung
Wardrobe design by Sophia Wu and Nausheen Sheikh

Cover and layout by Vikram Sangha
Common Core questions by Tracy Hualde
Reading level assessment by Tracy Hualde

ISBN: 978-0-9913194-7-3
Library of Congress Control Number: 2014920702

PRINCESS Ten Ten AND THE DARK SKIES

WRITTEN BY
SETSU SHIGEMATSU
& THE GUARDIAN PRINCESS ALLIANCE

ILLUSTRATED BY A. DAS

The Alliance

The Guardian Princess Alliance (GPA) is an organization committed to educating and empowering children to make a positive difference in the world. Our organization began as an initiative aiming to transform the cultural meaning of the princess. The Guardian Princess Alliance is a growing community of parents, educators, students, artists, and professionals who share a common goal of creating better role models for children through our stories and media.

The Guardian Princess stories represent princesses as superheroines who protect the people and the planet. Our diverse princesses model compassion and intelligence and demonstrate the power of knowledge and collective action. Our magical stories promote racial, cultural, and gender diversity. We hope this story will help affirm different gender identities and facilitate dialogues about how to prevent bullying. This new fairy tale is dedicated to those who don't always fit in and those who are working to take better care of our planet.

Acknowledgements

Special thanks to those who made this book possible:
Abigail Micu, Jr.
Alessia Belanga
Alice Barlow (Maw)
Allegra Rose Beadle
Jodell Usher
Kate Smith Scalero
The Keenan Sisters
Maia Keira Cabanel-Bleuer
Mark Driscoll
Mary Ellen Duke
Tiffany So-Lee

And those who helped the story along the way:

Craig Wiesner
Daisy Kim
Elizabeth Klein
Erika Suderburg
Gaetan Caron
Jane Ward
Jolie Chea
Krishna Das
Megan Van Der Toorn
Nina Smith
Nomi Lee

Pachet Bryant
Pia Palomo
Raja Bhattar
Rié Collett
Rob Delamater
Sandy Liang
Sarita See
Tei Okamoto
Tetsuro Shigematsu
Tracy Garcia
William Hansen

CHAPTER

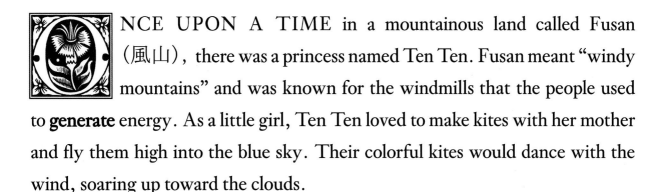NCE UPON A TIME in a mountainous land called Fusan (風山), there was a princess named Ten Ten. Fusan meant "windy mountains" and was known for the windmills that the people used to **generate** energy. As a little girl, Ten Ten loved to make kites with her mother and fly them high into the blue sky. Their colorful kites would dance with the wind, soaring up toward the clouds.

Ten Ten and her mother would sing:

> *Feel the power of the wind as it dances through the air*
> *Mighty and strong, yet gentle and fair*
> *Fusan! Fusan! Oh, the skies are so blue*
> *The beauty of the sky is a gift for me and you*

Ten Ten had lots of energy and did not like to sit still. Every morning, she would run to the temple to watch the boys train in martial arts. She was drawn to martial arts but had to watch from outside the gates, because girls were not allowed to train in this traditional practice.

The practice was called **_Tiandao_ (天道)**, meaning "the way of the heavens". Princess Ten Ten would copy all the forms by herself outside the temple walls. One morning, the highest-ranked teacher, Master Yun, saw her practicing alone. He knew that she was special and that she could become the next Wind Master.

Master Yun spoke to Princess Ten Ten's mother, Lady Mina, and asked permission to train her. Lady Mina questioned, "How can you train her when girls are forbidden to practice at the temple?"

Master Yun answered, "The old ways are slow to pass. With your blessing, I will train her myself. One day, she will show the world that it is time for change."

Ten Ten's mother replied, "If you are willing to train her, then please do so. I know that Ten Ten wishes with all her heart to study martial arts. All I want is for my child to be happy."

Princess Ten Ten began learning _Tiandao_ from Master Yun, practicing her kicks, blocks, and strikes every night under the moonlight.

Tiandao pronounced: Tee-ahn-DOW

From a young age, Princess Ten Ten did not act like the other girls. She always wore loose pants, which made it easier for her to practice martial arts. She felt uncomfortable wearing dresses. At times, Ten Ten did not feel like a girl, and she did not fit in with the girls or the boys. Other children of the court, like Yi and Chu, would make fun of her and call her names because she was different.

This bullying made Ten Ten feel scared and sad. But then she grew mad. She often told Master Yun, "I'm going to use *Tiandao* to get revenge on Yi and Chu." But Master Yun would always calmly reply, "Ten Ten, martial arts should only be used for self-defense and to protect others from harm. *Tiandao* is not for revenge." Even though Ten Ten tried to be strong and brave, she often felt alone.

King Wu disliked that Ten Ten always wore pants. He was embarrassed because even his court disapproved of his daughter's appearance. One of the court advisors named Li-Shu would whisper to the king, "A princess should not look and behave like this. Her hair is **unkempt**, her clothes are a mess, and she never wears a dress! That is not how a princess should represent Fusan." Li-Shu's cruel words turned the king's heart cold toward his daughter.

One day, King Wu scolded her, saying, "Ten Ten, I am ashamed to see how you dress and act around the court. Why must you act this way? You are not the child I had hoped for."

Ten Ten felt crushed, and tears welled up in her eyes as she said, "But I am the daughter you have. You don't understand me! You don't even know who I am!" As she spoke, her lips and hands trembled. Princess Ten Ten wanted to be strong, but inside she felt shattered. Her father's angry words pierced her heart. She began to wish that she were just like the other girls of Fusan who played quietly and only wore dresses. She wished that she was not so different and that the other children would stop making fun of her. She spent many nights crying herself to sleep. Lady Mina realized how much Ten Ten was suffering. She finally decided to send her daughter away to live with her grandmother.

CHAPTER

Grandmother Sun Hee lived beyond the mountains of Fusan. She was cheerful, wrinkly, and wise, and loved Ten Ten's free spirit.

Princess Ten Ten would often ask, "Grandma, why don't the other girls and boys like me? Why are they so mean to me?"

Grandma Sun Hee would give her grandchild a big hug and say, "Ten Ten, don't worry about fitting in with the other children. You don't need to be the same as the other girls and boys. You were put on this earth for a purpose—to be the special person you are."

While she stayed with her grandmother, Princess Ten Ten continued to train in the ways of *Tiandao*. She practiced all the lessons that Master Yun taught her. Each day, her body grew stronger, and she gradually mastered all of the secrets of *Tiandao*. With her grandmother's love, Ten Ten began to accept and love herself, too.

Back in Fusan, Li-Shu plotted a wicked plan to increase her power.
She would replace Fusan's windmills with factories that would make her rich.
She planned to use black rocks from inside the mountains to power the factories
instead of using the wind.

Li-Shu went to the king and convincingly said,

"Out with the old, in with the new.
Top of the line, only the best for you.
Big factories bring more power than the wind.
You will be the first with this new trend.
This is the way to have more power,
To make the workers obey, we'll build a watchtower.
You'll create jobs, and the people will thank you.
I'm sure the ancestors will be proud of you, too."

The king was hesitant at first, because he knew that the ancestors warned against using the black rocks. However, he could not resist Li-Shu's appealing words. Before long, he agreed to her plan and made Li-Shu his chief advisor. They ordered the workers to start building the factories right away. Other workers were ordered to cut off the peaks of Fusan's beautiful mountains to find the black rocks.

Soon, the factories were built, and Li-Shu ordered the youth to work in them. The workers were locked in the factories and burned the black rocks from morning to night. Billows of smoke and **smog** poured into the clear blue skies. As time passed, the elders and the children of the city began coughing and getting sick. However, their plight did not stop King Wu and Li-Shu from burning the black rocks. As they burned more rocks and grew even richer, the people became sicker, and the skies grew darker.

CHAPTER

Several years passed, and the Moon Festival was approaching. This was an important time for families to gather and celebrate the beauty of the moon and the autumn season. Grandma Sun Hee suggested that it was time for Ten Ten to return to Fusan and see her parents again. Princess Ten Ten was excited to be reunited with her mother and father. When she approached Fusan, she noticed that the skies over the city were now dreary and dark. The beautiful white clouds she loved were gone. Only layers upon layers of smog could be seen. She was shocked.

As she rode through the city, she could see that the people were sick and suffering. Princess Ten Ten yelled, "Stop!" to the royal rickshaw driver and jumped out. She asked the people, "What has happened to Fusan?!" They told her about the new factories and how burning the black rocks had made them ill.

After hearing the people's stories, her shock turned to anger. She ran to the palace as fast as she could and burst into her father's chambers.

"Father, what has happened to Fusan? What have you done? The skies are gray and full of smoke. The people are sick!"

Her father ignored her concern and said, "Ten Ten, I see that you are still wearing pants. Shouldn't you be preparing your dress for the Moon Festival?"

Princess Ten Ten insisted, "Can we even have a Moon Festival with skies that have become so dirty? Where is Mother?"

Her father said impatiently, "She has become ill. Ten Ten, you are too young to understand the power of the black rocks."

"I'm old enough to see that the skies are no longer blue and that the people are suffering," answered Ten Ten.

"Enough of your defiance. I will not have my daughter question me. Now, go!" King Wu ordered.

Princess Ten Ten left her father's chambers in frustration and went off to find her mother.

She found her mother coughing, wheezing, and struggling to breathe. Her once-radiant face was **ashen** and gray. Ten Ten had never seen her mother like this. She ran to her side and hugged her, crying, "Mama, why didn't you tell me that you were sick? I would have returned sooner." Lady Mina weakly whispered, "I didn't want to worry you. Do not cry for me, my child. You must be strong. You must go and help the people before it's too late."

She left her mother's quarters, wiping away her tears, only to run into the bullies from her childhood, Yi and Chu. They said in unison, "Princess Ten Ten, you're back!"

Yi said, "Have you seen what has happened to Fusan's skies? We really need your help!"

Chu said, "Yeah, Li-Shu locks the workers in the factories all day and all night!"

Ten Ten hesitated. Seeing them made her remember why she left Fusan.

Yi and Chu could see from her face how Ten Ten was feeling. Quickly, Yi said, "I'm sorry we were so mean to you when we were kids."

"We didn't understand you because you were so different," Chu added, looking down at the ground sheepishly. "We didn't know how to treat you."

Remembering her childhood made Ten Ten feel hurt and angry, but she also recalled the words of Master Yun and her grandmother. Master Yun taught her to channel her feelings into purposeful action. Grandmother Sun Hee helped her accept and love herself. She could now forgive the people who teased and bullied her when she was younger.

Her mother's softly spoken words, "…help the people before it's too late," echoed in her mind and heart. She knew that they would have to work together to save Fusan. Princess Ten Ten looked at Yi and Chu and said, "Our past was dark like the skies, but we can work together to clear the air. Let's do this!"

Early the next morning, Princess Ten Ten approached the factories. In the center was a concrete and steel watchtower where Li-Shu **monitored** the workers below. Li-Shu wore a frightening gas mask to protect herself from the air, which was thick with smoke and dirt.

Ten Ten climbed the locked tower and was soon on the roof. There, she began her *Tiandao* moves. She chanted:

> *The way of the heavens and the path of the wind,*
> *Be our source of energy, let us rise up and begin*

Princess Ten Ten began whirling her arms and hands to create a wind ball. She raised the wind ball and released it into the sky. The wind ball swirled and spiraled through the smog and smoke. The spiral in the sky signaled to Yi and Chu that it was time to move.

Ten Ten flipped from the roof and shattered the window of the watchtower with a flying roundhouse kick. Before Li-Shu could blink twice, Princess Ten Ten stood tall in front of her, broken glass at her feet. Shocked to see the princess, Li-Shu almost fell out of her chair.

Princess Ten Ten confidently declared, "On behalf of the people of Fusan, I order you to shut down these factories."

Li-Shu answered, "I have the king's permission to run these factories all day and all night. You can't stop me!"

Princess Ten Ten said, "Li-Shu, you have corrupted my father. You may try to stop me, but you cannot ignore the voice of the people!"

Li-Shu's eyes slowly widened as she heard the sound of clanging metal grow louder and louder. She looked out of the broken window and saw crowds of people marching toward the factories, clanging their pots and pans. Overcome with fear, Li-Shu fled toward the palace.

As the crowds of people approached, led by Yi and Chu, Ten Ten joined them below. Together they broke open the heavy locked doors of the factories that had kept the young workers inside. The workers poured out of the factories, overjoyed to be free. They all marched toward the palace.

CHAPTER

As the crowds of people approached the palace, they practiced a magical *Tiandao* chant that Princess Ten Ten taught them. For the first time, all the people were learning the secret powers of *Tiandao* that they did not know ordinary people were allowed to use.

They were met in Fusan's square by Li-Shu, King Wu, and his guards. Li-Shu declared, "Ten Ten, how dare you rally the people against your father! You do not know your place."

Princess Ten Ten replied, "Yes, I do. I'm here to protect the city and the skies with the help of the people and the winds of Fusan."

Li-Shu screamed, "Guards, silence her!" As the guards made a move toward Ten Ten, she ran and flipped over them, then jumped high into the sky.

She rose into the air, spinning round and round. From her hands, she released wind balls that created a small tornado. As Ten Ten spun faster and faster, the people of Fusan began chanting:

The way of the heavens and the path of the wind,
Be our source of energy, let's rise up and begin
Winds of the East, Winds of the West,
Help us protect the skies, we will do our best
We must work for what is right and for what is fair
We must stop the forces polluting our air
O great winds, heed our call! If not, our city will surely fall

The people's voices resounded across the square as they chanted and beat their pots and pans in rhythmic fashion. Young and old alike lifted their voices to the heavens. The vibrations of the drumming and the sound of the people's voices increased the wind energy of Ten Ten's tornado. It grew bigger and bigger, moving higher and higher. All of the people were united in their purpose to help Princess Ten Ten clean up the skies. As the tornado gained power from the people, its force sucked the smog and smoke into its center.

Finally, the giant tornado pierced through the layers of darkness, revealing patches of pale blue sky. Upon seeing this color again, all the people cheered and began jumping with joy. The blue patches grew larger, and the king stared in awe at what his daughter had done. He was shocked that she had become a Wind Master and that she had parted the smog-filled skies with her special powers.

As the smoke and smog disappeared, it was as if the clear skies brought clarity to the king's mind. The people of Fusan could breathe the clean air again.

When Princess Ten Ten landed on the ground, Li-Shu yelled, "Guards, arrest her! She has defied the king."

King Wu declared, "No! Guards, arrest Li-Shu!" as he pointed toward his chief advisor. King Wu continued, "Li-Shu, you **ensnared** me with your cunning words, and I followed you down the path of greed. We acted against the good of the people and ignored the warnings of the ancestors. I will begin my path of **penance** by asking the people's forgiveness. My daughter has the **Mandate of Heaven**. Therefore, it is only right that I now give her the throne."

The people gasped upon hearing this great announcement.

"Thank you, Father. I will one day become the next ruler, but now my Mandate of Heaven is even greater than being the ruler of Fusan."

Just then, Master Yun appeared from within the crowd and said, "King Wu, indeed, Princess Ten Ten has saved the people and the skies of Fusan. She shall become the next Guardian of the Skies. As a Wind Master, she will work to protect the skies of all nations, ensuring clean air for the next generations."

Mandate of Heaven: an ancient Chinese belief that the heavens allow
rulers to stay in power as long as they are just and fair

This is how Princess Ten Ten became the Guardian of the Skies.

With the skies clear again, the people prepared for the Moon Festival.
During the opening ceremony, Ten Ten looked **regal**, dressed in a specially designed red and gold pantsuit that gleamed in the moonlight.

Everyone could see that Princess Ten Ten was no ordinary princess.

ETYMOLOGY CHART

Etymology: the history of a word

Name based on Chinese characters	Meaning	Chinese *pronunciation*	Japanese *pronunciation*	Korean *pronunciation*
Fusan 風山	windy mountain	Feng Shan 風山	Fûsan ふうさん	P'ung San 풍산
Ten Ten 天天	heaven & skies	Tian Tian 天天	Ten Ten てんてん	Cheon Cheon 천천
Tiandao 天道	way of the heavens	Tiandao 天道	Tendô てんどう	Cheon Dô 천도
Wu 武	military	Wu 武	Bu ぶ	Mu 무
Mina 珉娥	beautiful, good, noble	Min-é 珉娥	Mina みな	Mina 민아
Sun Hee 仙姬	goodness & pleasure	Xian Ji 仙姬	Sen Ki/Hime せん き/ひめ	Sun Hee 선희

GLOSSARY

Ashen: having gray-looking skin due to illness or fear

Dreary: causing unhappiness or sad feelings

Ensnare: to trick and trap someone into a bad situation

Generate: to make or create something

Penance: an action you do to show that you are sorry

Rickshaw: a small vehicle with two wheels that is pulled by a person or a bicycle

Smog: clouds of dirty air caused by factories; a type of pollution

Unkempt: messy, untidy

Monitor: to watch or check something/someone over a period of time

Regal: royal

COMMON CORE DISCUSSION QUESTIONS

Designed for 5th grade reading level.

1. *Princess Ten Ten and the Dark Skies* is the first Guardian Princess Alliance book to explain how a princess becomes a Guardian Princess. Summarize how Princess Ten Ten is chosen to protect the skies of all nations. (RL.5.2)

2. The last sentence in *Princess Ten Ten and the Dark Skies* says, "Everyone could see that Princess Ten Ten was no ordinary princess." How is she different? Choose at least five adjectives to describe Princess Ten Ten. Use specific details and examples from the story as evidence to support your word choices. (RL.5.1)

3. Princess Ten Ten's clothes and behavior cause different reactions from the people of Fusan. Reread the interactions that Ten Ten has with Grandma Sun Hee. Now compare those with King Wu's reactions to Princess Ten Ten. Compare and contrast how both characters respond to Princess Ten Ten's differences. (RL.5.3)

4. King Wu has a very convincing advisor named Li-Shu. Reread her plan to build factories in Fusan on pages 14 and 15. Using what you know about Li-Shu and clues in the paragraph, determine the meaning of the words (RL.5.4) in bold:

    The king was **hesitant** at first, knowing that the ancestors warned against using the black rocks. But he could not resist Li-Shu's **appealing** words, and before long, he agreed to her plan.

5. Princess Ten Ten faces challenges in every chapter of this story. In chapter two, we learn that Li-Shu forces the youth of Fusan to work all day and night in locked factories. How does Princess Ten Ten respond to this challenge? Discuss at least two more challenges that Ten Ten faces, and use the text to explain how she reacts. (RL.5.1 and RL.5.2)

6. The beautiful illustrations in *Princess Ten Ten and the Dark Skies* help the reader feel the changing moods of each chapter. Look closely at the first illustration of Ten Ten flying a kite, analyze the illustration of Fusan on page 16, and now study Ten Ten on page 24. Discuss the mood in each illustration. (RL.5.7)

7. Determine the overall theme of *Princess Ten Ten and the Dark Skies*. Be sure to use key details in the story to prove your thinking. (RL.5.2)

ACTIVITY

Princess Ten Ten works together with others to clean the air of Fusan. Did you know that there are many cities in the world where the air is so dirty that the blue skies can no longer be seen? What can you do to learn about air pollution and how could you help improve this problem?

Color the picture below. Use the Guardian Princess pledge for inspiration to write your own poem or song.

We pledge to do what is just and fair

To do our best to protect and care

For all living beings great and small have worth

We shall come together to take care of our Earth

By accepting our differences and working together

We're able to keep our air clean, now and forever

We shall protect the seas, skies, and lands of all nations

To be cherished and shared by the next generations